LOSS

DAVID HARSENT

Loss
(white nights)

FABER & FABER

First published in 2020
by Faber & Faber Ltd
Bloomsbury House
74–77 Great Russell Street
London WC1B 3DA

Typeset by Hamish Ironside
Printed in the UK by TJ International Ltd, Padstow, Cornwall

A CIP record for this book is available from the British Library

ISBN 978–0–571–29055–0

FSC
www.fsc.org
MIX
Paper from
responsible sources
FSC® C013056

2 4 6 8 10 9 7 5 3 1

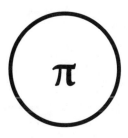

Square the circle? A poet might. None else.
FERDINAND VON LINDEMANN

LOSS

The city never sleeps   silence would weaken it
when all else fails it talks to itself   seamless thrum
of machinery   dark undertone.

It is 00:00 and the full of the night yet to come.

I

How would it be to live without whisky without wine –
an even tread in chequered sunlight? Or live without music
and nothing to fill the hollow of your heart? Poetry corrupts,
we know. As a child he gloried God with song and lived in fear.
He fell and was lifted up to fall again. He is lost now as then.
Women of the house – he lay in the dark and listened to their voices.
He knew they bled because he saw them at the wash, found blood
in the water-trap. Their talk was a constant, soft, overlapping,
under and over music, soft questions, soft laughter, diminuendo.
Or live without love, bones drying under your skin, skin
pulling back from fingerbones and cheekbones, bald at heel and toe,
your eyeballs gone to a crust, your arsehole a pinprick, all
for want of love. He knew they bled. It was magical, beyond him,
they said as much. Soft hands on him. God was in the reckoning.

There are false starts
as ever. There are words
as yet unspoken. There are
chances lost twice-lost.
There are fevers
under the skin. There are doors
opening on vacancy.
Without whisky without wine
diet of piss and pabulum
teeth loosening a debit

of flux no less than your due
long reaches of the night
given over to listening:
the footfall in the hallway
the cry from the garden
little deaths hidden theatre
those changes that go
unnoticed how memory weeps.
Unspoken heavy with truth
and sorrow. The way out
now lost doors opening
on vacancy or some kind
of timeslip heavy traffic
on the ring-road HGV
Class 8 dump-truck D-Max
Pickup music playing
(her late gift to you)
the head-on crash symphonic
a white dissolve though if
you look again it plays out
as a frame-by-frame-
slow-motion-light-show
cartwheel of sparks and parts
wet debris torn face
uppermost such dreams
as narrative not prophecy
as record not warning
the worst already with us
dogfight politics barrel-bombs
children scorched faceless
deluge and wildfire. There's

the puppet-clown virtuoso
of filibuster and farce.
His teeth chatter with rage
and glee his eyes rattle
in his head. And there's
the store-front whore
red-lipped wide-hipped
her figleaf basque
and fishnets purple lug-worm
veins on her inner thigh
yourself to yourself as you look in
herself to herself as she looks out.
And there's the demagogue
aut Caesar aut nihil
down to the footlights to take
his curtain call. The young
are ransomed the unborn gone to waste.

Quirks of history, the births of evil men, a sudden rise
in willing blindness among the best of us, some loss
of shadow. We live with it day by day, the one surprise
how vainglorious our response, how raw, how crass.

The dead hour of the night.

Drink to hand   fragments of a broken dream and sleepless
now   nudged up to this tall window   tree-lattice
moving on a livid sky   navigation lights   streetlights
moonlight flooding the cloudwrack.

A man out on his own   desert or salt-flat.

II

There are forms gathered in the sky that he takes to be angels.
He believes in angels as he once believed in unassailable virtue.
There are voices that can't be accounted for. There are faces
that come and go. There is a fool let loose in his house
which explains the breakage and wreckage, the faecal smell.
There are rooms in his house that he has never seen.
His heart went like a songbird's fast and light, morning delayed
nonetheless. He got up and walked about, a man in waiting.
He sat down somewhere, a chill on the place. It seemed clear
there are rules that cannot be broken except by death
there are slums out of which comes greatness that goes to waste
there are things that fall to hand but can never be kept
there are chance meetings that discover a turbulence of love
there are maps that will take you to the edge of things.

As you put your hand
to the latch of the garden gate
your foot finds the void
a soundless blue unseen
untried. Faces that come and go
a troubled sleep blood
on your fingers but how?
Heartache presenting
as heartache a sense
of unease as if something

had shifted or spoiled standing
day after day before Bacon's
Fragment of a Crucifixion that
and Bonnard's mysteries
of domesticity a room empty
of all but the chair
where you sat to read
or be read to the soft
yellows of Candlemas
attendant slow music
that even now bears down
on you as if forgiveness
might be allowed and even now.
That such things come back
to you that night-
fears are a loop-tape
that faces paper your walls
that a fathomless blue
is the purest and worst
of dreams that voices of those
you once loved (now loveless)
speak to you out of silence
that silence fills the room
that you live alone
in that breakage and wreckage
and the music she gave you
be heard day and night
that it plays with rainfall
double-drumming that you sleep
in the reading-chair
and wake after years to find

nothing changed your mood
as it was and still there
the note you wrote to yourself
on the back of your hand
a wind tumbling trash
in the streets mad men
in full bluster the turning
wheel of bad news death
squatting still on Yemen
its children given up
to fire (and fire it will surely be
fire now and fire hereafter)
as they wait in the rubble
for rescue for water
for the blood-wagons
the loop-tape the music
voices out of silence.

A late sun throws shadows on the lawn. Things shift
to find perfection, patterns of leaf and birdsong, soft
arrangements that masquerade as gift
in memory, bliss delayed and love a kind of thrift.

A silky thread of illness   dark damson smirch   fruity
smell   something gone soft at the joints near-disarticulated
imagine its slow crawl   flop-flop-flop up stairs over
floorboards   seeking seeking . . .

The dead hour   false city light   light of illness
glow of pollutants overripe   nickel-cadmium-nitrogen-oxide
breathe in breathe in   they settle and corrode   pallid
moon utterly out of place   green flashes spike the sky
ignis fatuus airborne.

A man out on his own   salt-flat under moonlight white on
white   the sky bears down on him   small dark figure
wholly alone in the whiteout   is he lost?

III

The way of candlelight with bare walls, hidden theatre
truth and sorrow on an indrawn breath, the weight of belief
his lode of Pentecostal plunder, the test of accidental sin
the promise of retribution (*Salve me!*) in the hope of which
he walked for days in hill country, pilgrim of crest and ridge
trading on the certainty of rough weather, singing
into the fullness of a gale, eyes fogged by distances
the wind singing back to him, benison or so it seemed
and what he carried all he owned, all he would own to.
He came back and they took him in, soft hands, he shrank
from their scorn, from their love, he ate what they put out for him.
His sleep was blackout, too deep for dream, near-death
or so he liked to think. He would go to the gate and open it
and set foot as if walking on air could be an act of grace.

Lost then gone to ground
yourself and God in hiding
(*Praise him! Praise him!*)
stout men turning
to one another with open
smiles as they sang
eyes lit by certainty a shine
to their cheeks a bloom
and women shoulders back
their faces formed

to the descant the swell
and shrill of it touching them
everywhere yes but endless
darkness underfoot
a shift in the floorstones
shudder of something
on the rise as might have been
the same pitch that defileth
as might have been
a disturbance among the dead.
You stood among them
pipsqueak fixed on the naked
Saviour stock-still on the cross
gone deep into his sadness
a man of sorrows
and acquainted with heartbreak.
A certain word you had found
stayed with you: say *forlorn*
say it for the savour say it
under your breath say it
to open hidden doors as curse
or riddle to find meaning
in the music hear it
in the long-drawn-out-
come-and-gone of a car
passing your window
at night ventriloquism
of wind women singing
as they worked one
fluctuating note needle
and thimble each stitch

a tiny devotion (*Salve me!*
Salve me!) and there you stand
face to face with the warrior
returned a man heavy
with truth and sorrow
his wounds and sudden silences
tragic beyond you unknown
or better say unknowable
whether in black and white
or Eastman colour
faces in torchlight not his
clouded by smoke not his
in grime in grease not his
bloodstained not his
with a hard stare with bright
blue eyes and meat-eating grin
not his but O a face
of broken lines a face
that would never own itself
or heal and you turning
your back as if to darkness.

The desert prophet says things will end in fire.
Men of science, too. Scribes and crystal-gazers, fire
the sure prediction. Red skies, the pitch and howl of fire-
storm, barrel-bombs falling through it, fire feeding on fire.

Rain slow at first then gathering speed and weight
trees carry the weight   the sky a grey-green blur
a bruise of cloud round the moon.

To watch this   to sit at the window still holding the
dream-fragment   desert perhaps   an endless
stretch of white sand or salt-flat   a man on his
own   is he looking for someone?

IV

Rooms in the house that he has never seen. A door
opens on this – the women at table, a place
among them left for him as if it would always be that way.
A blessing on the food, plates going hand to hand.
The ritual calmed him to the point of sadness. He learned
all food is sacrament, he learned the rhythms of gossip
he learned how gesture and glance were narrative, that song
was their true language, that silence held all of this.
He spent time by the window. It would mist and clear.
He wrote in the mist. He talked to himself in whispers.
He put himself among them to listen and watch, the way
a rabbit might be hulked and jointed, the way it spilled
the way it was praised and preferred, soft hands gloved in blood
the room a black chapel then, the song, the sacrifice.

No pretence to live without
pleasure whisky music sex
whatever guilt depends on
her fallen clothes or else
the memory of that:
a sunlit morning bedroom
how it clouds with sin
as you bring it back
trading off the verb *to gorge*
soft shock of bodies

meeting in what seems
shared malice but of course
is fear words failing flesh
falling into debt. Why
is there no way back?
Don't watch as their mouths
open on each other don't watch
as they take each other's hands
for their own. They are wrapped
in white light the long mirror
gives them back to themselves
as arranged they make small
donations one to the other
of joy and sorrow in equal parts.
Be sure they know how it plays out
be sure her eyes will close
on the last of him his on the last
of her denial taken and given.
And they'll come back to this
as versions of themselves
the same exchange the same
excess trade like for like
vouchsafe the same small lies
hope for sunlight as it was
because none of this endures
in darkness will remember
what names they gave
what they might do what they did
to encourage each other
the way their bodies made shapes
in the cheval-glass it will be

the best of before a refinement
but far from perfect far
from what they need from what
they have in mind which most
resembles the lissom flow
of a hare over rough ground
the long low glide of a hawk
as it quarters rough ground.
But they'll be lost to this
bound up in themselves a closed
fist in a closed fist she'll turn
her back to him he'll turn his back
to the mirror's broken sunlight
the hare on broken legs the hawk
trailing fire the turning wheel
percussion and slow collapse
scorched earth the dying flare
of winter ice under a winter sun
vision of skyborne angels.

Finally, silence which has its own song to sing.
The stone-dead heart of stone, the heart of glass.
The collision of nothing with nothing.
What absence would be if absence could be less.

Wind working the rain   the garden sways in grey
the house leaks   open the window the air has a
cordite smell   is tepid   sharp reek of illness
again.

The dream-fragment is no more than this   no less
white sky white landscape   a man stranded there
unmoving caught between white-on-white
impossible to say what will become of him.

Slant rain sculpted to furls and rolls by the wind
the garden awash   a noise like hammers or else
the deep hammer-beat of the heart   blood-pulse
near-musical.

V

There were dead things at the tideline, scooped up, brought back
laid out for burial. 'The sea gave up its dead' – he wrote it down.
They gathered stillness. They could not be understood.
He sat in the shade to read; he sought true loneliness; he thought
stillness and loneliness might be found in 'the *very depths* of the sea'.
He wrote it down, he wrote down 'fathomless'. A shallow grave
ritual placement of pebbles lifted from the beach, he knew
they would go to rot, he knew 'decay' as like to 'burden of sin'
and that his name was logged. Faces in cloud, voices in wavebreak;
he read the signs that prompted him to prayer – unbroken line
of sin and sacrifice, shed tears, shed blood, the call for recompense.
He would go bareheaded in penance, go barefoot over the stones.
'God gives and God takes back' – he wrote it down
word for word – 'Naked I came and naked will return'.

Some terrible black
machine its motor grinding
and churning pistons
cranking *slam-slam-slam*
tracks hurdling whatever
they hit it is steel it is blind
it carries unheard-of
firepower things fall or ignite
before it this came in dream
and then again the second

night and now you sit
with your double
Tanqueray and watch it
come out of the blue
techno-perfection full-on
pinpoint strike and the whole
town goes to slow collapse
and you lean back
to her touch as she puts
her hand on you and you
have nothing now to say.
No chance of a refill between
this sequence and the next:
death-in-real-time-smart-bomb-
drone-strike-Xbox-incoming-
crosshair-sweet-spot-wipeout
the dirty dust-pall-shape above
the roofscape and voices call
Salve me! Salve me! everything
broken as in your dream streets
gone to rubble paramedics film-
crews women on their knees
the dead children dead children
her hand on the nape
of your neck. And now as you
open your mouth to hers
you feel you might
have outlived yourself as if
you walk from room to room
street to street always to slow
music the wrong man

in the wrong place the ghost
of yourself draped across
your bones. You dream of
engines of car-crash gunships
unloading although last night
yes it was snowfall
on moorland dazzle
of daylight-snowfall
drifts blurring Hound Tor
and Hay Tor unless it was
just a white dream nothing
visible touchable breakable
and you in that thickening
mist going sightless and trackless
as if you might somehow reach
a place of safety the Peaceable
Kingdom coming into focus
that first full view of it
like to stop your heart.

There's music that will not dissipate, it hangs in
hanging rain, fills empty rooms, belongs
only to nightfall and daybreak, brings in
what was unspoken and unrevoked and wrong.

It's clearer now   the way dreams come back to
memory   the man has been walking for days
caught up in white   no way of telling how long or
how far   flat sky unchanging   flat landscape
unchanging   nothing to register movement
nothing to measure movement   no sun no moon no
birds no hills no watercourse no track.

Dawn is a smudge   birdsong through rainfall
trees drifting into focus.

Here are the mysteries   little accelerations
how light pushes through   how the world shapes
itself.

VI

How would it be to live without hope or regret, for love
to be nothing but gain, driven and unaccountable? A wind
shuffles the curtain, his mouth opens to hers,
pericope adulterae, the woman is thrown down, Christ
draws in the dust with his finger, kabala kabala . . .
The congregation hymned and wept, they stood
shoulder to shoulder, they dropt to their knees. He learned
that joy is jeopardy, that prayer is capture. Gospeller
God's automaton, stigmata a hidden bruise beneath the skin.
Dull images in the mirror bring her back, first light,
gash-red in the sky and ochre, virulent, a storm below
the skyline waiting to break. She turns in her sleep naked
and open, her face wiped clean, her body raw to the touch
though he *touched*, all and everything given over to chance.

What's lost has gone to waste
immutable unless the dead
can claim their own. The river
trundles its hundredweight
of bones early morning glare
bonding the backwash nothing
of the man who went arms out
to the midnight tide-race of how
the bridge-lights came back
off the water broken reflections.

See that? The way he's gathered
and covered. See that? The way
others like him gone in the head
line up at the iron balustrade.
To fall that far to be lost
in thought a long soft glide
the night sky clear the surface
almost unreachable . . .
Bankside trees are tiring
in the wind. See that?
Your double is walking just ahead
contemplating a life without you.
Wrong to be here wrong to think
of turning back but think
of turning back imagine
a white bird on a blue sky that
sweet negativity or else
your shadow cast in the dust
a black absence yourself
as patterning that it goes
slant to you as it must that
it cannot be other than itself
despite the way you wag
your head the way your arms
hang the tilt of your walk
that it must come with you
to the edge where tideline trash
is wallowing in a slick
of sunlight scum of pearls
and silver trinkets.
The river moves in silence silent

singing which might appear
as a slow disturbance a long
shiver on the skim voices
that call from the riverbed
in unison perfect pitch it would rise
to your outstretched hand
and shake you into song.
The river is paved
with chequered sunlight lies
walkable. One step another step.
How far are you now
from home? Will they take you in?

There are those who walk in silence as they must.
They are envied. We step aside to let them pass.
What becomes of them? They go between the press
of earth and sky and scarcely shift the dust.

Crowd-noise of rain   a battle-roar   if only this
came in under darkness as it should but the city is never
dark.

Sleepers down in doorways in sidings under bridges and
tower-block wasteland   children's playgrounds
given over to dealers and dogshit   the rain will find
them out.

There was more to the dream   something dark
where the skyline should have been   something
moving fractured by the haze:

sleep now . . .

VII

A door opens on this still life of fruit and flowers, contraband
cigarettes, a medicine bottle of bathtub gin, bootblack mascara
bartered lipstick – tableau in a blind house; so if someone came in
if she angled the make-up mirror to find her face, if she sat
between two lamps as her shadows gathered and fell
one on the other, if she took her time, if she kissed herself
in the mirror . . . The house assembles round such gestures
stilled and held. Imagine, re-imagine – the fire stirs in the grate
the clock picks up, there's music from a room beyond that room
and voices much like music, deft rhythms of gossip, scandal
laughter, offhand profanity. What they say has been said before
but never by them and never like this. Cards or quilting
hands on the overlap fluent and fine. A radio tuned to the news.
Subtle hierarchies, bloodlines, notice of war and the war-dead.

It is fast and unforgiving it is
the way fear arrives in the guise
of gift a 'night-time visitation'
in which the car aquaplanes
in a downpour on the ring road
Cantigas de Santa Maria
that clear pure line and light
pours in rain an avalanche
fire rising fast through that
and you think how beautiful

a fusion the way colours
stand off each from the other
but somehow mingle all
come close enough to see hear
feel a vision glorious and you
the centrepiece airborne
turning in a turning wheel
of clutter and flame-mandala
but also in dream-geography
out on the hard shoulder
or else a bridge so you see
the pattern clear the way
it comes apart the way
it gathers and goes to stasis
'Crash Pattern in Blacks and Reds'
you breathe fire in the drench
even as they line up to watch
as the camera-crews find focus
as *Garda-nos* holds its own
that sweet unbroken line
the roar-and-rush of collision
kept at one remove although
a heartbeat will bring it in
to shock you awake but not
yet no you must see it
through as blood finds
the crevices flesh shreds
bones break and your face
in close-up wears the familiar
I-told-you-so look
of the puppet-clown and then

as you float arms flung
to the oncoming air it seems
you might reach out and find
her caught up in it caught up
in the dream turning shrouded
in flame in water her mouth
opening on yours as if to say
love could do no more
than bring me to die
in the moment you die my eyes
will close on the last of you
yours on the last of me if you
can hear this let me know.
Which is where it breaks down
here just short of Death Valley
awash burnt-out but still a place
of reckoning the Devil's rockface
God's monument.
                    A blue-white
light at the shutters. The dawn wind
carrying stingers of ice.
                    Garda-nos.

Holy men were stript and burned. Their flesh
shrivelled and glowed. The sky was empty then
of smoke and cries. A wind drew shapes in the ash
annulus, *vesica piscis*, flaws in the economy of pain.

The city is feverish   rivers run under it
they suppurate   they spill green.

The rain lets up   contrails hang and disperse.

Reflections in the glass   the world indoors shifting
the world outside   books pictures a face in close-up
as if a mirror had slipped its silvering.

VIII

Fool has left his handprint on the wall in candle-smut
above a scribble of hokum and filth, fools' kabbala.
Tricks of the trade – disruption, spoilage, spite, past-master
making undercover raids from cellar or attic, wherever
he's holed-up, happy to live in darkness among the discards
himself a discard, dab-hand at mayhem, artist of disquiet
he rehearses a Bacchanal, poses in fright-wig and blackface
as Lord of Misrule, the nude in 'Nude Descending',
goes from mirror to mirror admiring his goaty good-looks.
The house shuts down; windows darken; doors slam as if against
high wind, high water. Fool channel-hops – a house on fire, a man
comes out holding in his arms a burning child, the sky is black
with metal. A house on fire, a man comes out, he's burning,
the sky is black and red. Fool grins; there's lipstick on his teeth.

A green wound that you love her
as you do. She walks a step or two
ahead her voice comes back
half-heard she brushes
through shadows that flow
towards her snag her arm
seeking attention and you turn
your face away as she turns
wanting to be sure of you. Perhaps
she is leading you to a place

of consolation perhaps this
has happened before perhaps
it will happen again (*it will
happen again*) she listens
to heresy she pledges her very
soul she plays Eurydice come
soft-footed to the gates of hell
trading whispers with the dead.
Birds drift across the window
white on blue silent and slow
thought-lines of delirium.
You drink you channel-hop
slam-slam-slam wavebreak
against the door her mouth
opening on yours then
some kind of timeslip where
she is your hostage
your interpreter. She goes
naked in shadow knows how
to unlock to set foot the shades
stand in her debt they have
a need to be comforted
they'd bed down with her
if they could. If you listen
for it you'll hear the same
music gentle laughter
the overlaps of gossip they fold
into a waking dream that gathers
as song and will not let you go.
Naked in shadow soft hands
on her arm something of love

unexpired as it might be a mist
of rainfall as it might be
a breeze out of nowhere
moving so slowly it lingers
on her skin. The dead go by
in half-light. They sing inaudibly.
How strange to feel their lightness
settle on you to watch
as she intercedes to hear still
the dull percussion
of a rising sea. At the window
somehow a white bird on a blue sky

A gift held out and taken, a kiss given up and taken,
burden of the last look back, the last word spoken,
the likeness of the sky as if the sky might darken,
broken images set next to what will next be broken.

Wake to last light   the day gone   whisky to
hand   a creature goes through   dog-fox
sniffing out spillage   songbird's alarm-call
trees resolving to silhouette   this happened before
pretend that it can develop or change   pretend
there's another way.

There's no other way   its lesson is how to suffer loss
how to give back what was gained by chance.

IX

If it became impossible to touch and be touched, to see
and be seen, to love and trade ecstasy for risk where risk
is ecstasy, to be hidden in plain view, to be perfectly lost
which means lost to the world, lying side by side arms linked
in a bond so intricate it could never unfold or break.
If it became crucial to live out of sight, to be housebound,
to walk a beaten path in the garden, to sit at the window
blurred by rainfall, to sit barred and blocked, books
set aside that would never be read, rolling news of flashflood
and fire, angels treading the updraught, a chaos of voices.
If dreams should give the rest of it – the path in the garden
going underground, flood and fire as God's only gift
the house holding its secrets, that pattern of locked rooms,
what lies outside (voices, angels) crowding the perimeter.

You could make an installation of it
(and why not?) on a bare floor
in a bare hall under neon strip
what seems thrown down what seems
heap after heap of discards but is not
hair and shoes and spectacles
and clothes (teeth also saved)
repetition such that it blurs
images folding into one another
abstract just shape being evident

except this shoe except
this lens catching the light which is
error or artefact something like
iron litter carefully thrown down
by Joseph Beuys but more the bright
grotesque of Bacon's *Fragment*
of Dubuffet's *L'Arbre de Fluides*
what's torn what's wrenched apart.
Heap after heap grainy footage
of a cattle train snowscape
smokestacks scratch orchestra what
more do you need . . . dogs . . . what more
do you need of this the train
all but silent in snow footage
of carcasses thrown down naked
you could make a montage of it:
quick hands a low sun deepening
to yellow by trees and towers
the way shadows are cast the line
you need the shapes you need
a sureness of touch to bring it all
together perhaps a light-box
fragments and fractures backlit
and all of a piece not least
the new dead they lie
in a scatter your focal-point
they make sudden broken
angels in the snow.
Fool steps up. His art is palimpsest.
He'll tag your work spray-paint
a ditzy orange bug-eyed frog

at the door of the charnel-house
colour the snowscape blue redact
the chimneys configure the train
with silver-and-black chevrons
a snake drawn up to the iron gate
his name for this *Evil is as evil does.*
The frog spits bile. The snake
is hollow-eyed. He adds
speech-bubbles to the cold still air
'Hosanna Hosanna Ho—sa—*nna*'.

Children in a pool of light, a pool of dust; the way
images deceive, the way time shunts and stalls, a test
of what gathers and corrupts, what will not stay
as words unspeak, as children are lost to light and dust.

Pretend the river can be seen from here as it darkens
along its length   it's at the full   there are
patterns drawn to its surface now at nightfall   there
are voices almost unheard that lie on the skim   river
feeling the bedrock feeling the draw   its tides drag
like a bad marriage.

Sleep on and off sitting up.

What moved across that field of white left tracks
the man had gone   the dream gave in to white.

X

Walk five miles, walk ten, don't look up, bitumen blacktop
engines and sirens, raised voices, clatter of bin-lids lifted
by the wind, shop-windows passing his reflection from
one to the next, a man pushing on, pushing on, head down
looking neither this way nor that, swimmer in foetid air
caught up in his thoughts perhaps perhaps thoughtless
he knocks shoulders hard with some in the crowd, a woman
cries out, he hears it as like a cry from the foot of the cross
still holding above the din, it's Holy Saturday and Christ
will harrow hell as advertised. Here now. The church
is well-lit and full of sound, not as it should be not as it was.
He sits. He goes to his knees. Stupid that he falls to weeping
stupid that he tries to call on God, that his body seems to shut
down in sight of the crucifix. Winter nightfall. He goes
out into darkness; the city unmapped and turbulent.

Lost life is fragments each untried
each glimpsed-and-gone except
they reside in thought someone
turning away raising a hand
speaking and unheard or ignored.
Anger is the one sure thing
or passion which you know to be
anger's best outcome. You seem
to go back to back with hurt

unwanted visions unwanted dreams.
How did you come so soon
to those brutalities to music
that calls them up to lines
that bruise the heart but come
so late to the one true thing
you cannot have? Night-thoughts
tend to death your parents buried
one atop the other your mother
fed daily through a straw silent
she lapsed she died you saw yourself
an artist making a sketch the bony
nose the fallen face mouth scummed
with shadow pen and ink a dull
lemon wash that being the colour
of illness (and that the scent) snowfall
at the graveside no one
spoke no one wept but there came
a massive stillness to the air
it seemed your blood checked
in its flow it was nothing
like loss or desertion a long
high note held in the round
of your skull nothing like
a cry nothing like song nothing
like the shrill of a trapped animal
it was itself alone and perfect
to the moment the sky pale
and fractured nothing
like glass nothing like ice topsoil
and snow shovelled back in. O allow

those bleak histories allow wastage
allow that depth of dark laughter.
Books fall open to the page
where they were last abandoned
music stalls in the mind faces
in photographs shift lost life
you dozing over her letter
with its codes and sly geographies
disturbed in sleep by that seamless
sound which is nothing like brake-lock
nothing like metal on metal nothing
like the sound of a weeping wound
nothing like your slipstream as you fall
through plain air nothing like
the uninterpretable voices of angels.

Discover the crash-test dummies waiting in line.
They smile at sacrifice. They are broken for us.
Glad to be chosen, glad to be loveless and nameless.
Dry-eyed they go to the gear and die without stain.

Fever scent the night-wind cannot shift   the city's
constant   a fox noses the trash   same fox.

Micro-sleep brings micro-dreams   a dark place
a door opening and closing   a dog going through
(what might have been a dog).

Voices up from the street in rage or surprise   a
streetlight blinks on and off . . .

XI

Now he must come to this room, 'the gallery', images
lost to memory long since, one something like
Bacon's *Fragment* hung close to something like Bonnard's
La Fenêtre (but none had seen that view or read that book)
a fleshy nude arse-up, a bird too hung with feathers to be skyborne
(talons deep in the dying) a pastel landscape of The Peaceable
Kingdom (phantasm and ruse) angels riding the firestorm
high above Death Valley where burn the unredeemed (wordplay
on sinner/cinder), 'Portrait of the Artist As a Flayed Head' (bald
eyes in a weeping wound) 'Judas Crucified' (his tallit spread
like wings to catch the wind). O let the room settle
in silence as before, shuttered, abandoned, everything here
given over to slow effacement; let the figures on the cross
(especially those) smudge and blur, darkened by cataract.

A swell in the river water
heaving onto the banks as some
behemoth puts its shoulder
to the flow subterranean
roar shockwaves turning
the tide *behold he drinketh*
up a river and treads the bedrock
breaks through the berg
of detritus backwash
of broken things vast head

of horn and naked bone
breaking the surface eyes
fixed on the pinnacles
and towers the monuments
and monoliths of the prim
and pestilent walled-in by money
who will enchain anyone bring
anyone to a bad end even those
few you love must love
from a distance no help for that
and his force is in the navel
of his belly his press a tidal bore
taking upstream a terrible
wild shout *vox dei* not words
of warning but words
that gather to a massive
seismic pulse beating
on bridges to bring them down
on stone and steel on glass
on timber to bring down
and wash away fire
swarming in the midst
since fire may burn on water
and the creature comes up
out of the flood to go among
the wreckage its body doused
and burning. O there will be
scorched earth tsunamis
charnel houses blood-pits
a plague-wind unless you put
a stop to this. Come back

come back to yourself allow
it is calm on this stretch
at dusk light fades along
the surface as if gathered
to the skim late birds set
a dull reflection and you
no more no less than the rest
harrowed pursued
by night-fears by fear
of what cannot be changed
or shunned or denied
or owned-to in silent prayer
mortal sin the neat systematic
hell of *hortus deliciarum*
abandonment of love.

Because they are burned in effigy, the good and wise
because the despicable can turn on what they most despise
because the *lingua franca* translates as lies and lies
and lies again, the blameless go always in disguise.

Night never finds true darkness or moonlight or starlight.

And there's something wrong in the way silhouettes
gather and fudge their true shapes.

And the whine of traffic fits the whine of the wind.

And the sun will later push up through a wash of toxins.

XII

Memory warps all things, *ergo* he lies to himself
without wanting to. Memory is wastage. Memory justifies
loss to anger, heartbreak to recklessness. Memory shows him
a place of silently closing doors, a web of hallways
a garden closed off to sound, a painting (dimly-lit)
of the risen Christ, a bureau that holds letters and photos
left by people he will come to know. It is pitiless.
He was leader of a bully-gang. He near-strangled a boy
with his own scarf. He stole and denied. He confessed
to be rid of blame: 'For all have sinned and come short
of the glory of God'. He wrote it down. When he ran away
the police brought him back. He had about him stones
and feathers and a jam-jar for fishing tiddlers. He was flogged.
Alas and alas. His hatred of them was boundless.

Somewhere trackless somewhere
in a wide white space you will come
into yourself as a circling bird
broad-winged dreaming your flight
sleeping or dazed or dead
the soft heft of the updraught
tilting your wingtips. Can you
see yourself can you imagine
how it would be to give yourself
over to deliver yourself to that

endlessness of sky to slow
dissipation while others
stand naked to be judged
(*Salve me!*) all hungers gone
herded and penned ankle-deep
in the embers of their sin?
In this imagining there's fire
what seems a gathering wind
is the tumult of the lost rising above
the inferno's pitch and roar.
Dark angels attend it. Is this
what you want to hear? What else
do you need to know of last things
of soul-sleep deliverance Christ
to the blameless pagan the *vesica
piscis* his shroud vulva of Our Lady
the soak of her birthblood.
In this imagining skies darken
they shrink from that. (What is fear
of the dark but hunger for God?)
In this they shuffle their feet
and wait in this they troop
on and down without a backward look
in this their names obliterate in this
they ignite as chaff and hold
a steady flame. Is it that you want
to risk the Creator's unforgiving gaze
and you dry-eyed despite
what couldn't be called back
or cancelled or denied? Do you think
white nights absolve you

or passion's sacrifice? Let go all that.
The bird flies endless circuits
going through walls of white it waits
to be absorbed by white now white
is earth and air seas pouring white
on white the sun a white monstrosity.
So you will come into yourself
white-eyed nothing to ask for
nothing to surrender.

Rat-spawn and night-hag go about their business.
The world has need of them. Their shadows fade
before they can be cast. Don't ask forgiveness.
One carries a bag of bones, the other a naked blade.

The nightscape is broken by what seem pits of light
are windows   are beacons   are where the city's
true insomniacs court their demons.

The way enemy fires might start up and be counted from
the ramparts.

Here is more whisky   here is one of the many unread
books . . .

XIII

That men love battle, that war backs up to war, that nations
fall to evil he knew. That loss is usual, that sorrow comes
as weather comes – unstoppable – he knew. That the century
is mired. That grief is common music. That nature is pillage.
That minds can warp as iron warps in fire he knew.
He would live in a clean place, water close-by, bright scarps
of outcrop rock and thornbush, hard-cut horizons, a wind
to scour and scarify, landlocked and no way back.
See it as he sees it – bring in a hawk quartering home ground
or some small startled thing turning in the shadow of itself
a mirage cupped in your hands or set under glass
albedo moons, knuckled landscapes, frost-fall . . . That it would stay
only on a held breath he knew. Soon there's a thread
of smoke along the skyline, carrion-birds riding the drift.

Because memories of sin
and loss renew and multiply
it must be whisky and fasting
so you can hear your own
confession so you can reach
and touch yourself hand on heart.
Who else could hear you? Who else
could touch you? Who could
be told such secrets as run
in the blood that drum in the pulses

of your wrists? What memories
wash in? What sense of shame?
What flashbacks to slippage and farce
that whisky can't dispel
what face it will not blur? Think back
(since now you must) to the telltale
smudge of blood on her fingertip
(to the smudge of blood) to rooms
ringing with silence to words
spoken/unheard to some small
gesture lost to indifference
and then a slideshow: twilight
under trees a door seeming to close
then closing folded hands the last
train its gallery of dead reflections
and again Cranach's *Expulsion from
the Garden* a view of Kristallnacht
from an upper window and again
a treeless plain holding points
of light in utter darkness ('human
torches' the caption) mirrors
set up to trap whatever strays in
(this called 'tyranny') and again
landscape-barely-landscape
near-colourless sky and skyline
lost to one another (titled
'blank canvas' or 'vision')
and again a shape underwater
rising against the swell
black-backed and soundless
(given as 'dreamwork').

Full glass and empty bottle
the perfect match and you
fallen holding onto the floor
wearing that sweet smile
of surrender music playing
windows open on the night.
Here's to the end of it
to the dregs to the last
last chance to the stumble between
soil and soul to the scissor-line
below which go your name
and age (also your *status*) O
here's to the white screen
(edgeless) and the chorus-in-memory
as you seem almost to wake.

Consider the stonefish, its shuttered mind, its one
purpose to poison, to poison and kill if it can.
As it goes to the heart and head so it goes to the bone.
The stonefish parable is grace through pain.

Driven rain across the window   a fusillade of light.

If the wind picks up much more there will be wreckage.

Chaos is nature's only true response.

XIV

His heart laid red and wet on one pan of the scale, a feather
dropt on the other. A door leads to an ante-room dimly lit.
Cabinets hold grave-dolls and trinkets, all the lost things
now come to light. Beyond a second door, a passageway
in which the air will be less breathable and he become
less visible as death is incremental. His negative
confession *I have made none to weep* he gave bald-faced
whereat the gods pulled back and stared. This is not now.
He goes through the day-by-day with nothing much in mind.
There are small rituals to be upheld, small words to be spoken.
The countdown to mild oblivion is this glass and this and this.
Living in dream he clothes his shadow-self. One night
he will open the second door to catch his last look back
fading between bare walls that draw together in the dark.

The ground beneath your feet
you will allow and have said so.
The sky you will allow not rooms
that shelter echoes not the road
into the wood. As before memory
bewilders you its gains and losses.
Black on white you will allow
that much is sure. White itself
untouched you will allow
on days of abiding melancholy.

There is pattern in time and event
that defeats you now and always
a stillness in objects laid down
and left to themselves your pen
your razor some keepsake long
ignored as stopped music
is stillness in air as a painting
will draw back into itself. Books
you will allow not loose words
that fall to misuse to a shout
to a closed fist. Failing light
through trees gives the illusion
of skyborne faces looking in
but benign watchers and keepers
pledged to protect. It might be so
and you will wake to a day
like any other hard frost low sun
long shadows river at the brim
all blurred as you would want
sorrow and guilt and loss to blur
become the one deadweight
you must hoist to your back
like any navvy as labour is virtue
as the work of hands is holy
or so you believe as you believe
that if things said to be ordinary
are taken for what they are
barely nameable barely
touchable it is one of the small
miracles (*Salve me!*) that go
everywhere unseen. Confession

and prayer you will allow not
forgiveness forgiveness is waste.
Perhaps you realise how far
you live from the complexities
of joy how far from delight
walking ankle-deep through
a rubble of discards of wrong
choices of words to the wise.
How tempting to fall
to your knees. There is
commotion crowding in
mad music tin-lid coloratura
loop-tape love-words engines
breakage attack-dog chorus
the rush (for all you know)
of a wind from Paradise.
Why not sit here quietly back
to the wall drink in hand
hoping to see things out? Why not
give in to heartbreak? Visions
you will allow not prophesy.
Light through trees you will allow.

A mother with her child, blood and milk, the street
in swift collapse, folding and falling; this holds
as the camera requires, as the fireball will also wait
for scorch and stain as the rest of it falls and folds.

Things judder and slip as if the night doesn't know how
to pace itself.

Flash-dreams are image and sudden movement then
gone   one is a figure at work on something that
can't be seen   another might be a creature in motion
low-backed   another still a man coming through a
door and about to speak.

The sky clears   there's a half-moon fogged by
dampness in the air.

Look:

XV

A hallway of doors. How will he choose? Take the seventh, take
the thirteenth, take the first, the last, the one that opens onto a room
where the mother and the father sit at table, hands dipping
this dish and putting this with that, helping themselves to that
and that (and that). Their heads are bowed to the task
but soon they'll look up. He'll join them and it will be wordless
nor will they smile. The father breaks bread into his soup. The mother
is busy about her lips with a patterned serviette. *The pity of it.*
Red meat puddled in blood, a jug of cream, all as it was
and windowless, bare walls, trinkets on every surface, every surface
scrubbed. *The pity of it.* To breathe the same air takes all he has,
to watch the pattern of hands, to translate the unsaid. Fixed in time
but timeless. Nothing to forgive and all things unforgiven.
The silence deadens. He shuts his eyes. Still here   still here   still here.

In reckonings of loss she comes
soon to mind in the way
gestures make shapes in air
the way nakedness is gesture.
Warm winters smell of death
you heard her say as much
then say *It will come to harm*
meaning some defenceless thing.
When she leaves the room naked
her shape is held in air her voice

is held as if her going were chance
her warning an afterthought.
It's all guesswork. The wind shifts
she goes to scrying a pebble
in her mouth quartz veins
making her spittle fizz road-kill
opening up to a gut-hook-knife
or she sets facing mirrors
where she will turn and turn
in white-lipped silence until
she blurs and falls the mirrors
holding her double image
eye to eye in the full of her collapse.
She will lose herself in memory
like any refugee. She will open doors
and step through naked as if
nothing might come of that. She is
the pickpocket of dreams
the dramaturge of mood-swings
she can be lost to you then found
as you turn away turn back
while she tells you how the sea
took on a deeper swell
as she watched how a cutting light
shuttled across the skyline and how
things could come apart (she opens
a book at a marked page)
the seam in the sea unpick
the skyline lift and tear
(she hands you the book)
her smile a blood-bruise.

She draws for you: a rat
in a skull sharp-eyed dark-eyed
and writes 'Your Lifelong Friend'
she draws a house and writes
'House of Hallways and Doors'
a portrait that is you but might
be anyone although she writes
your name and that is capture.
Remember how she stood
face out to a moorland wind
wanting to taste it? She touched
herself delicately then
knowing she was watched.
Image and voice all there is of it.
You could see the rain coming in
from miles away. When it hit
she went to ground like a hare
to its form wanting some measure
of darkness. She might as well
have been in that same room
curtains drawn door locked.

Here is the stylite penitent weathered to a wick.
Here is the *mysterium tremendum* which is vapour
which is mirage which is pabulum to the soul-sick.
Moonblind and mad; rapture beyond cure.

The window-glass shakes   a helix of reflected light
trees dance on darkness   a face but featureless
shadow of clouds   double shadow   all these
shift and collide.

What's wrong is the shadow-shapes   the wiped face
how trees mark the sky.

Wrong.   Wrong.   Wrong.

XVI

His small-hours city-walk, he high-steps in the half-light
a sodium drench on the M-way approach roads, a soft
sick glow in lanes and back alleys and short-cuts. His eye
is trained to detritus, to what's left or lost or broken
or abandoned or scorned or forgotten – a trinket
or glove or snapshot or letter or brooch or doll
or a news-sheet thrown down and trodden into the wet.
He has a shelf for such collectables. They will become
a collage as per Rauschenberg, that 'visual flux';
there will be ersatz blood-drips holding one thing
to the next. (Or this is a fever-dream in which he talks
to the dead and goes in the guise of a prophet haloed in ash.)
A wedding snapshot, yes. The news-sheet is sodden. He peels
the front page from the rest. ALEPPO   ISIL   BATACLAN.

What would you set aside
to have what you most miss?
Don't think of that. There falls
a shadow-crucifix across
the river-path crowcall
from the bankside trees.
Omens-not-omens ooze
from a poison-garden
blackwater runoff broken
glass this feather-and-bone

spillikin underfoot. Don't
think of that. Don't think
of sudden blindness the world
continuing unwatched
you in your doorless cage
of missed chances arse-out
to the hoi polloi acting
re-enacting the shilpit the gowk
your dribble-and-gibber routine
your dodder-and-drool.
What would you set aside?
Fog on the water slow deep
tidal draw. The bridge-rails
leave frost-burns across
your hands which is stain
which is ice-wound
which is omen enough.
Will you feed on yourself
blood and gall and gash
in your cage of broken glass
and bonewrack where
you can neither sit nor stand
neither call nor cry?
The glass-shards catch the sun
which is whiteout which is flood
of cataract. It's said
that you barely sleep.
It's said that when you do
you dream the cage-dream
and wake with bite-marks
on your arm or dream

a man plays knuckle-bones
with his scarface double
or dream an insect (shiny black
carapace fuse-wire legs red
pin-prick eyes) that opens
the skin behind your ear a neat
round bloodless hole and sets
out for your heart going
by way of your eye. And
O there's the dream
where she comes in wearing
the pelt and poll and snout
of a she-wolf and curls up
at the foot of your bed.
What would you set aside?
Patterns in sleep merge
and pull apart reds and blacks
alarms a muddle of voices.
Images pool in your head. A man
is falling he missed his step
on the last tread of the stair
and now he is falling through acres
of air at terminal velocity
deafened by his own slipstream
as his eyeballs roll back as the roots
of his hair smudge with flame and no
dreamstock-turnabout no flights
of angels now to bear him up.

White figures in a white room, they are speechless.
This is the draft of a scene from a drama called 'Loss'.
Stage directions call for gestures of distress.
White stalks white, soft-footed, murderous.

*The lamp flickers sending a swarm of shadows to the
walls.*

A songbird starts up fooled by the city's false dawn.

*Here is the glass frontier between the world indoors and
the world outside.*

*In the well-lit streets of commerce and calumny the last of
the lost bed down.*

XVII

He'll be baffled by pain, that's his best guess. He calls up
images of frame-by-frame diminishment and wonders
how he might see it out. Put with that the scream on scream
of a mating vixen or the long weep of a buzzard, anything
that memory stores as solace which is also of course regret.
He shuts his eyes; the object becomes the moment, portrait
of a woman (that *freggio* cut deep into her cheek)
a white canvas, rubble from the gutter laid in a shallow box.
They go from room to room, he taps her hand, she reaches back
to find him, he's close behind sharing her line of sight,
she catches his reflection in the glass, he gives a gentle tug
to her hair, she kisses him and there's the spit from her lip.
Effacement he thinks, the way smoke ravels and pulls
apart on a day so still that death is a disturbance.

        You tried to keep pace
        with the year the year
        outstripped you tyrants
        took hold the world
        became world-weary
        and the weak sickened.
        O dark laughter
        from lost souls from jails
        and whore-houses from
        asylums from the new

dead who turn their own
soil and mutter requiems.
This is what it is to hear
voices crossfire of cries
and whispers you go
shaken into the streets
kerbsides silt up with
the dumb distracted
then come sounds
like razor-wire birdsong
like blood-rush like bone-break
and a figure in freefall
at the far edge of your eyeline
which could be an angel
with clipt wings could be
the first of the airborne
suicides. Then only bad blood
and dreamless sleep. It's cold
and the light is going. You sit
unmoveable a man
in lockdown your breathing
slow and shallow heartbeat
a bare echo. Imagine your eyes
taped shut your ears stopped
that blind silence is trance.
She enters naked unmarked
a stone under her tongue.
she carries news of things
laid waste of fire on the skim
of the sea. God bears down
on the world his voice

breaks rocks and the skies empty.
Nothing to do but offer up
all you have nothing to do
but offer what you love.

Siege machines crank up in some suburban street.
The blind tap-tap to the wire and wonder what.
At the pavement-parallel light and shadow meet.
It hangs on a single shout, a single shot.

Someone going by at a flat-out run   Muybridge's
'fight-or-flight' sepia-toned under streetlights.

A waning moon when the clouds pull back   there are
shapes in trees   night-raven   cockatrice.

Sleep–wake–sleep   white on white behind the eyes.

XVIII

Glory in sacrifice, agony in the garden, kiss for kiss, the gift of blood.
He is taken with this. Taken with 'Christ and the horrors'. Taken
with love and betrayal: *Judas went out and it was night*. In that
moment came Christendom. Whisky-hunger nags him. Confusions
of memory and desire. (On certain subjects no more can be said.)
A day when it rained without let up, the fragrance from gutters,
he wrote it down, that trees rolled in the wind, that everything
was monochrome, river and sky and street, that the roar and thresh
of rain-in-the-wind locked him off from himself. He sits quietly now
head dropped O in a soundless trance, the house falling still
as if focused on his stillness, a drawn breath, the heels of his hands
pressing on his eyes as the dumb-show goes frame-by-frame
forms merging, pulling apart, shadow-play of sin and redemption
in which he ransoms his soul, is held to account, is taken down.

In that dead silence
she turned to hold you
in the blaze of her eye.
Whatever's spoken then
can't be unsaid. As you know.
Light on the water
is a knife to the whetstone.
You'll find rime
on the bridge-rail
unmarked and bird-tracks

in the mud your long
shadow lost among
the shadows of trees.
That confusion delivers
remnants of dream
a doorless gallery a painting
of a book a snuffed candle
a cut rose another
in which a dog-pack
is on the move blur
of brindle snouts low
to the pavement eyes wet
with streetlight a third
which gives a replica
of the house you once
knew and forgot where she
enters stage left bringing
a mirror which she holds
up to you image/imago
and enters reading a letter
that she will sometime
burn to stripe her face
with ash and enters to become
herself-not-herself
'Nude in Sunlit Room'
where the painter took
from the rise of her breast
to the bevel of her hip
a line that has the exact
meander of a tear-track.
Beyond that image

white walls take the light
drift and slippage where
the dream gives way
but music lies under it flush
as a bruise lies under skin
did you hear it slow
notes and blood-creep?
Check the crook of your
elbow the back of your knee
it goes to hidden places
plays on your long bones
settles to grow darker.

They use words wrecked of meaning; they draw
their weird from the day's detritus; they show
themselves for all the world to see: skinned raw
eyes peeled, worm-cuts from which their new selves grow.

A flight of stairs a corridor a room a window   how
things change moment to moment   how grey moves
against grey which is onset dusk which is failing sight.

Reflections in the glass turn on and off   sheet-
lightning or power-jolt or apnoea.

At 3 a.m. memory turns sour which is small fears
returning which is dream-feed which is absence of
prayer.

XIX

This room now, papers and books, a long drift over tables
over chairs to the floor. She said, 'You'll find him here
up to his arse in the tar-pits of poetry, find him lost
in some landscape of the mind, the mind's perfect drear
salt-marsh-as-moonscape-as-snowscape-as-white-over-white
which is limitless from skyline to skyline.' She said, 'There
are ghosts here that crowd and jostle; they feed off silences
and wait for nightfall.' And, 'I will turn cards to find
what's left for him, what's left for me.' With that,
a shift in her womb – the unnamed child. Sometimes
he lies down with these rejects. His finger-bones ache;
he imagines them blacked by a lifelong seepage of ink.
Among the crosshatch of deletions one line untouched.
She said, 'This comes not from the scar but from the wound.'

She is the girl waiting
at the crossroads about
the dead hour of the night
in the face of *fiers magyk*
and whispers from the gibbet
ready to haul you down
and hold you fast no matter
what ugliness you come to.
She is your lost bride
and the heart's failsafe.

Full moon in midwinter stillness
is death in abeyance
as blood slows and you
are held in that pale light
frost-fall and a caught breath.
There is no true healing
not at the well of sorrows
not at the whipping-post not
at the communion rail
(Christ's firebreak) not in
the hall of mirrors where
you are set to rights
not in the basement bar
where you sit down
to a whisky-chain
and fall and rise and fall
back into a raw dawn light
over high-rise slumland
whose people each new day
go blind to daybreak
numb to the toxic wind.
You know too well
their turf-war battle songs
their live-by/die-by graffiti
you know their stopless need.
Somewhere far from this
a cloudburst hits
the clitterfield. A hawk
rides the thunderhead.
It is sure evidence of grace
that stones glow

in a tarnished light
that the sound of the sea
pushes back against
the sound of the rain
that she can bring you here
with a gesture that sets
you and stones and bird
in the churn of the weather
and the arc of the sublime.

Prayers are raised against havoc and harm.
Tyranny goes by another name.
Word is sent from the sightless to the dumb.
The storm-horse gallops through the fire-storm.

No sense of daybreak   no measure of daybreak   no
call for daybreak in this lapse this long fermata   breath-
stain on the glass forms but doesn't fade   all else deepens
all is undiminished as sound remembers itself   as traces of
light throw a pattern and take hold.

Everything fixed on the tip-side of destruction   scree of
detritus   street-slops   dockside trash-heaps
echoes from the world indoors are tesserae of troubled sleep
dim night-music of syllable and slur.

The moon is set in a circle of light.

XX

How would it be to live without this press of words –
set loose in the world to no purpose? He would play
pitch and toss with the Old Man, cold and clear-eyed
or carry his coffin to the market and set up shop
trading in toys for the Day of the Dead
sugar skulls, grave-dolls, a bony bride and groom
in their cerecloth finery smiling gap-toothed smiles.
Fool has a gappy smile of his own and a hotline
to the women of the house who appear as handmaids
of Santa Muerte, wearing that same wartime wardrobe
same pompadour hair. They whisper one to another
and glance across trying to put a name to the face.
He lies down limb by limb by limb. The grave-dolls
should have corsets and bee-stung lips. He writes it down.

What do you see what
do you see now? White
birds on a darkening sky
they cut their own
shapes as they roll into
the wind. Small visions
come and are lost. It is
cruel that falling away.
Dreams reassemble a face
come close enough to kiss

tarnished by something
much like a scorch mark.
Put your fingertip
to that naevus trace
on his back the delta-web
of scars he got
from the lash of God
O a fallen angel
has business with you
(have you woken?)
he shows you what
you cannot bear to see
then shows it again
he speaks in tongues
he opens a door on this:
women at the stove
or at the sink passing
a song between them
on this: a child reading
and crying on this:
(have you woken yet?)
a bed in a room set up
for night-watch and
endurance of pain
on this: storm-glare
silvering a valley unless
it's the sea unless a steel-
and-black-glass cityscape
on this: where she stands
holding your likeness up
for the world to see as if

you might be recognised
and found on this:
an emptiness that is nothing
but white on white your eye
blanched by it heart
in jeopardy to it the bowl
of your skull holding
a cold white light that rings
against the bone. Now you wake
to unbroken stillness
out of the dream stillness
and a deep numb silence
as after snowfall as after
violence and the birds
locked off against the sky
and the near world become
touchless and everything
held on a fault-line set
to fracture just where
you kneel buck naked
and given over to God.

Here is the man himself, his scars and sores.
There is nothing good to be said of him. He meditates
on the effect of pain but never on its cause.
He can no long tell what he loves from what he hates.

A man out on his own   desert or salt-flat there's the dream.

Another night but trees wind moon as before   as before
whisky the unread book the streetlamp's halo of toxins.

And ghosts as images in the glass   reflections that
arrive without prompt or purpose   women pausing to look
up   lost to sorrow.

Diesel and garbage and fast-food   jet-fuel-shower-city-
sewer-smell   scent of illness airborne as if the hospitals had
tipped and spilled.

Tower blocks jigsaw-lit   tail lights   night-creatures in
parks   in side-streets   they go nose down to the trash.

Moonlight locks the garden under ice   or it's a lake of
black floodwater   fish swim in that translucence swim
in that groundwater-swill   they are sightless and slick-
skinned   this world's first and last.

Moonlight out of cloudwrack shed from the cloud's edge
midnight sky a tarnished blue.

Moonlight and streetlight and pockets of deep dark that are
alleys or city scrubland   thin-white near-black   nothing

is what it seems   love and dreamlife and symptoms of regret
all in parallel   themselves and not themselves.

00:00 and the full of the night yet to come.